Welcome

We are so excited that you've chosen to join us as we journey through Daniel together. This six-week guide is designed to take you deeper. Each week, you'll find five daily devotions to help you learn how the life of Daniel applies to us today. We've also included a study guide with discussion questions for your small group. All Bible references are from the New International Version(NIV) unless otherwise noted.

There are resource links provided on page 94 and throughout the study. Use these if have questions or are ready to take the next step in your relationship with Jesus.

LET US KNOW HOW YOU'RE JOINING THIS STUDY BY SCANNING THE LINK BELOW.

As a church, we have been preparing to deep dive into this study and are so excited to journey with you.

Many hands and minds were behind the scenes making this happen, but we want to give a special thank you to Kathy Ferguson, Torrie Sorge and Dominique Donesing for the writing, editing, research and layout of this project. Also, a big thank you to Traders Point CC for providing the study guides included.

We know that each contribution will help strengthen our journey as we find ourselves "Among Lions."

TABLE *of* CONTENTS

HOW TO LOOK UP A BIBLE VERSE

WEEK 1
12 DAY 1 | **14** DAY 2 | **16** DAY 3 | **18** DAY 4 | **20** DAY 5

22 STUDY GUIDE

WEEK 2
26 DAY 1 | **28** DAY 2 | **30** DAY 3 | **32** DAY 4 | **34** DAY 5

36 STUDY GUIDE

WEEK 3
40 DAY 1 | **42** DAY 2 | **44** DAY 3 | **46** DAY 4 | **48** DAY 5

50 STUDY GUIDE

52 WEEK 4
54 DAY 1 | **56** DAY 2 | **58** DAY 3 | **60** DAY 4 | **62** DAY 5
64 STUDY GUIDE

66 WEEK 5
68 DAY 1 | **70** DAY 2 | **72** DAY 3 | **74** DAY 4 | **76** DAY 5
78 STUDY GUIDE

80 WEEK 6
82 DAY 1 | **84** DAY 2 | **86** DAY 3 | **88** DAY 4 | **90** DAY 5
92 STUDY GUIDE

94 RESOURCES

HOW TO LOOK UP A *Bible* VERSE

1. IDENTIFY BOOK

To begin, identify the name of the book located at the begining of the verse reference. Then, find that book within the table of contents in the beginning of your Bible. Once you have located the page number for the book, turn to that page. In your Bible, the name of the book will appear at the top of the page.

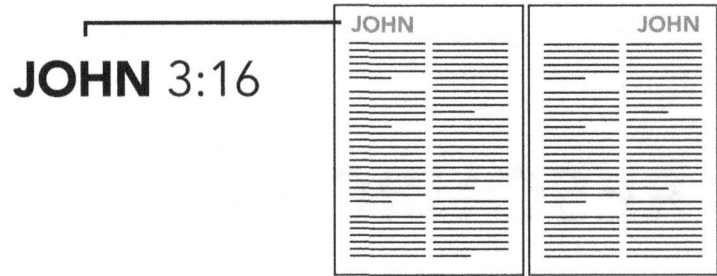

2. IDENTIFY CHAPTER

Once you have found the correct book, identify the chapter. This is the first number that occurs in the verse reference. In your Bible, the chapter number will appear as a large number at the beginning of the chapter.

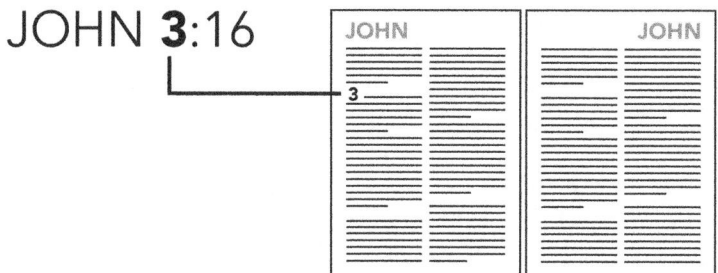

2. IDENTIFY VERSE

The final number in the verse reference identifies the verse number. In your Bible, it will appear as a small number located at the beginning of the verse.

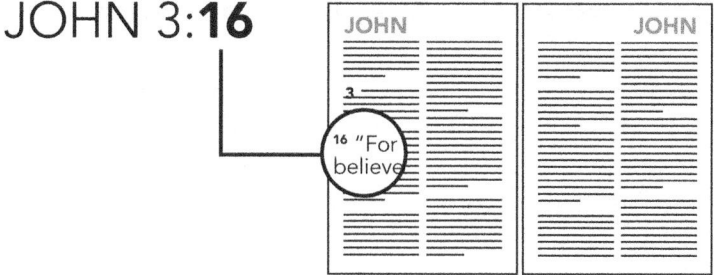

Among Lions:
WHEN CULTURE SHIFTS

Context: After defeating Jerusalem, King Nebuchadnezzar takes captives back to Babylon including Daniel and his friends.

After decades of war and destruction, Jerusalem and her people find themselves broken, with very little hope. They don't even have a temple where they can worship. It would appear that God has abandoned them. It's here, in 605 B.C. we find four young men, Daniel, Mishael, Azariah, and Hananiah. The four, along with many others, had been taken captive. After his victory over Jerusalem, King Nebuchadnezzar of Babylon took those who possessed strength, beauty, and wisdom, leaving the weak behind.

Being forced from your home, friends and family after watching the destruction of your beloved homeland had to be painful. But we will see that these four possessed something far greater than the outward characteristics the king rewarded. They had an unwavering faith in God they carried with them. It was their foundation of faith that they would stand on when their circumstances looked unbearable and impossible.

> *"Jesus Christ is the same yesterday, today, and forever."*
> **HEBREWS 13:8**

We also can have that certainty of God's love and care if we focus on Him and His principles for our lives. It might seem impossible to love God more than your family or friends. But when we make God our first priority and build our lives on Him, we're able to face unforeseeable hardships, struggles, and challenges with peace. So, what does faith like that entail? First, it begins with submitting completely to His Son Jesus as we ask Him to forgive our sins and accept His gift of salvation. It continues with daily devotion to God through prayer, worship, Bible reading and listening for His voice and direction. God is available to everyone as a loving father and companion who welcomes us into His arms through times of mourning, pain, and suffering. We can take comfort and courage knowing that the same God Daniel and his friends relied on when their homeland, family and all other forms of familiarity were snatched away from them is the same God we can trust with all of our circumstances today.

Thoughts

1. Think about a challenging time when you suffered pain or discouragement. How did you see God intervene to help you heal?

2. Examine your own faith. When hardships come, are you quick to focus on your circumstances, or seek peace in God's love?

3. Write a prayer to your Heavenly Father asking Him to help you grow and strengthen your faith as you learn to trust in Him day by day.

Context: Daniel and his friends begin living in exile in Babylon.

Have you ever been afraid of the future? Everything in your world seems unfamiliar and you're not sure what to do. Maybe you're afraid of choosing the wrong path. Or maybe the decision is out of your control altogether. Fear sets in, overwhelming your mind and body, holding you prisoner.

Yesterday we read that Daniel and his friends endured years of war and destruction. Now they were faced with an uncertain future in a foreign land with an unfamiliar culture, language and customs, many of which contradicted God's laws that they'd been taught to honor and live by. But, King Nebuchadnezzar demanded full compliance. Daniel and his friends were prisoners. They didn't know what the future held, but they knew they weren't in control. Their lived experiences to that point would have made it easy for fear to take over. They were already physical prisoners. Fear would have made them emotional ones as well.

We've all experienced fear of some kind: an accident, diagnosis, the loss of a job or loved one, or uncertainty. The way we respond makes all the difference and is a clear indicator of how deeply we trust God with the details of our lives. Daniel and his companions learned that their only comfort and guidance would come from God.

> *"Have I not commanded you? Be strong and courageous. Do not be afraid; do not be discouraged, for the Lord your God will be with you wherever you go."*
>
> Joshua 1:9

In the days ahead, we will see Daniel and his friends choose to be courageous in the darkest moments in spite of how they feel. Does that mean they weren't afraid? No. Being courageous isn't the absence of fear. It's trusting that God's promises are true, that He is who He says He is, and that He will never leave us.

Thoughts

1. When have you found yourself in an unfamiliar situation? What concerned you the most about these changes in your life?

2. Think of an area that you are currently fearful about. What would it look like for you to completely trust God with it?

3. Write a prayer honestly sharing your fears with God and ask Him to replace your fear with His courage and peace.

Context: Daniel and his friends are given new names after entering Babylon.

Names are foundational to our identity. Some hold deep significant meaning while others are passed down generationally. Think about your own name. If someone decided to suddenly start calling you by another name, it would feel uncomfortable, wouldn't it? This is what Daniel and his friends faced shortly after arriving in Babylon.

In today's verse, we find Daniel and his friends being assimilated into the culture. They enter a three-year training program indoctrinating them with Babylonian language and literature in preparation to serve King Nebuchadnezzar. It's at this time they're also given new names. Daniel is renamed Belteshazzar, Hananiah - Shadrach, Mishael - Meshach, and Azariah - Abednego.

Imagine, not only being physically taken from your homeland, family, and friends, but piece by piece every fiber of who you are is being replaced. How do you hold onto who you are? Or do you throw your hands up, surrendering to those who are in control? Once again we see why it was so important that these four knew who they were and Who they belonged to. Their faith and trust in God was so strong that even renaming them didn't shake their identity!

God also has names describing His unchanging character. For example, Jehovah-Jireh means "The Lord will Provide" (*Genesis 22:14*), Emmanuel is 'God with us" (*Isaiah 7:14*), and Jehovah-Rapha translates to "The Lord who Heals" (*Exodus 15:26*). One of the most personal names of God is Adonai which means "My Lord" (*Ezekiel 16:8b*). That is what God desired of Daniel and his friends, to be the true Lord of their life. Even when the king was stripping them of their identity, attempting to become the ruler of their lives, these four knew without a doubt that God was their Lord and He alone held their allegiance and devotion.

This is what God requires of us too. We might not have a king trying to literally rename us, but we do have society, culture, and social media fighting for our attention and threatening our identity. Just like Daniel, we too have to decide where our identity will be grounded and who or what will claim our allegiance.

> *"You shall have no other gods before me."*
> Exodus 20:5

Thoughts

1. Think about your own name. Does it hold significant meaning? Why or why not?

2. God desires to be the Lord of our lives. Examine your life. Is there something or someone that is more important than God? What would it look like to prioritize God as the Lord of your life?

3. Write a prayer of confession, repenting for the area(s) you haven't surrendered to God, and ask Him to help you honor Him in all things.

Context: Daniel and his friends are faced with a demand that they eat Babylonian food. This is their first big test.

How do you live in a culture where your values are constantly being challenged? How do you hold onto God when everything around you is pulling you in the opposite direction?

Throughout the Bible, we see examples of Godly men and women who lived within cultures that resisted God and his ways. Joseph, Lot, Ruth, and Elijah lived within cultures that didn't worship God, but that didn't sway their own personal commitment. It didn't sway Daniel's either.

In verse 8, we see Daniel and his friends make their first public decision to follow God. Until this point, their resolutions had been internal commitments. But now they were being served "royal food and wine." What's so bad about that? Israelites (Daniel's people) lived under God's law which had specific dietary restrictions. Perhaps the king's food violated these laws. Or maybe Daniel and his friends didn't want to show any loyalty to the king. Either way, they committed to eating only vegetables and water.

As we've seen over the past three days, Daniel and his friends had already determined to be faithful to God. While it's easier to resist temptation when you know what your convictions are, we still need God's help to overcome them.

> "Watch and pray so that you will not fall into temptation. The spirit is willing, but the flesh is weak."
>
> Matthew 26:41

God gave Daniel both wisdom and protection as he negotiated with the king's official. He didn't raise his fist in rebellion and shout, "No! I won't eat your food!" Nor did he demand everyone follow his convictions and values. He calmly offered an alternative, which gained him credibility and more importantly honored God. Like Daniel, we too can negotiate without compromising our values. Daniel approached the situation with respect, humility, and an alternative solution. With God's help, Daniel and his friends were able to be both respectful and uncompromising…and so can we.

Thoughts

1. Where are you currently tempted to violate your values?

2. When have you been able to negotiate a situation with another person without compromising your values?

3. Write a prayer asking God for His wisdom, help, and grace as you stand firm in your faith.

Context: Daniel, Shadrach, Meshach and Abednego are selected to serve in the king's palace.

Everyone has an authority figure in their life. Children have parents. Employees have bosses. CEOs have board members. Athletes have coaches. Some authority figures are likable and easy to follow while others are difficult and present a challenge.

Yesterday we saw Daniel and his friends' faithful, uncompromising devotion to God. Today we see their submissive attitude to the authority over them as they learned about Babyloian literature, culture, and language. Merriam-Webster's dictionary defines submission as "an act of submitting to the authority or control of another." Often submission is considered a weakness. But as we've already seen, these four were not physically, mentally or spiritually weak.

As captives in foreign land, it would have been easy - understandable even - for Daniel and his friends to allow bitterness, anger, and resentment to produce a rebellious and defiant attitude. However, if they had, they would have missed the blessing God had in store.

> *"Humble yourselves in the sight of the Lord, and He will lift you up."*
>
> **James 4:10**

Although they didn't know it yet, God had a plan. After three years of preparation, God blessed them with a greater level of understanding. In fact, King Nebuchadnezzar chose them to serve in important roles in his palace because their wisdom and knowledge surpassed everyone else. God's blessing was a direct result of their willingness to surrender to the author He had placed over them. Promotion was never their motive. Obedience to God was.

Next week we will see how God continued elevating Daniel's position and influence as he continued to live a fully surrendered life.

1. Think of the authority figures in your life. Are you harboring any bitterness, jealousy, anger or resentment toward them that is making you unable to submit to them?

2. What motivates you? Advancement? People pleasing? Validation and praise? Popularity? Obedience to God? Examine why you choose to submit to those in positions of authority in your life.

3. Write a prayer asking God to forgive you of any impure motives and help you humbly submit to the authority figures in your life.

GROUP STUDY GUIDE

Among Lions: WHEN CULTURE SHIFTS
WEEK OF OCTOBER 15, 2023

Synopsis:
The book of Daniel is a roadmap for how godly people can thrive in a godless culture. Daniel lived for God in a way that was winsome and influential. He didn't just survive the godless culture around him. He thrived in it, got promoted in it, and was viewed with respect and had influence within it. While Babylon tried to indoctrinate him, Daniel held onto his distinctiveness and didn't compromise his faith.

WARM UP QUESTION:
Share about a situation or setting when you felt like an outsider.

DISCUSS:
• What are some ways that you see culture shifting right now?

• What is typically your gut reaction when culture shifts: freak out, blend in, or hold onto faith? Why?

READ DANIEL 1 TOGETHER OUT LOUD:

Options: Split up the passage between 2-3 people or go around the circle, reading one verse per person.

• What stands out to you in the circumstances portrayed in verses 1-5? Is there anything that strikes you as particularly unfair or hard to understand?

• If you were in the shoes of Daniel and his friends, what would you struggle with as you're brought to Babylon?

• What stands out to you in Daniel's actions in verses 8-13? What does it reveal about his character?

• Have you ever found yourself in a situation where you were pressured to compromise your values? How did you handle it?

- Where or when are you most tempted in your day-to-day life to blend into culture or compromise what you know to be true?

- As you look at Daniel's actions, what inspires or challenges you personally in how you can respond to an ever-shifting culture?

- Do you have a "line in the sand" like Daniel did when it comes to holding on to your distinctiveness and not compromising your faith? If yes, explain. If no, what difference do you think it would make in your walk with Jesus to draw that line?

RESPOND:
- Based on what you've just discussed, take a couple of minutes to quietly reflect on a good next step to help you stand firm in the midst of a shifting culture. What is God prompting you to do in response to the shifts that are affecting you personally?

- Share with your group what your step is and when you will do it. Then spend a few minutes praying together, that you would each anchor your faith in Jesus and not only live, but thrive, in the current culture that surrounds you.

*Encourage group members to read Daily Bible Reading on the church app or have it delivered to their inbox daily. Subscribe at **www.thecrossinglv.com/app**. Check in with your group to share thoughts about these throughout the week!*

LEADER NOTES: Access to weekly message, podcast, & notes at www.rightnowmedia.org

Among Lions: WHEN PRESSURE'S ON

Context: King Nebuchadnezzar calls on his magicians and astrologers to describe and interpret his dream.

Have you ever felt tasked with doing the impossible? Maybe your parent(s) or boss has unrealistic expectations for you. You're confronted with their request, given a time frame and left to figure out the details, and failure is not an option. For some, the challenge is invigorating, a chance to prove yourself, while others are immediately overwhelmed by fear and pressure.

Last week, we saw Daniel and his friends choose to live fully surrendered to God despite their fears. In turn, God found favor with them, elevating them to highly influential positions in the kingdom even while still being captives of war.

Now we find the king has called on his magicians and enchanters to do the impossible – both describe and interpret a dream without any details about the dream. Nebuchadnezzar challenged the wisest men in the kingdom to help him understand the message, but they're quickly overwhelmed knowing what he's demanding is impossible. In turn he sentences them to death until Daniel steps in to assume the challenge and save them.

He and his friends immediately prayed for God's mercy and wisdom. They didn't rely on their own strength, intelligence, strategy, influence, or leadership. Only through God's revelation would Daniel be able to describe and interpret Nebuchadnezzar's dream.

When faced with challenging situations or circumstances, we're tempted to rely on family, friends, therapists or social media for the answer. While all of these are good and have their place, they shouldn't supersede seeking God. Often, it's not until we've exhausted every other avenue, wasted valuable time, and become desperate, that we finally turn to God.

> *"Trust in the Lord with all your heart and lean not on your own understanding; in all your ways submit to him, and he will make your paths straight."*
>
> Proverbs 3:5-6

Daniel understood that God was the source of wisdom. We don't have to know all of the details, predict the ending, or depend on our own strength, wisdom or ingenuity to accomplish impossible goals. It's when we learn to lean on God's wisdom rather than our own that our faith and trust grows and we become more spiritually mature.

Thoughts

1. Think about the last time you felt overwhelmed by a task or decision. Where did you instinctively turn for help? Friends? Social media? Google? Spouse? God? Why did you choose that resource?

2. What keeps you from fully trusting God or seeking His wisdom first? Why do you fall back on your "own understanding"?

3. Write a prayer thanking God for His wisdom. Ask Him to help you as you learn to rely on Him to direct your steps.

Context: Daniel asks his friends to pray with him for God's mercy.

Yesterday we saw that Daniel was faced with an impossible task, to both describe and interpret King Nebuchadnezzar's dream. We also learned that he relied on God's wisdom and not his own. Yet, today we read that as soon as Daniel leaves the king, he immediately goes to see his friends. While this may seem like a contradiction, it's actually part of God's wisdom being poured out.

Daniel knew he couldn't achieve this task alone. He didn't gather his friends to strategize, gossip or complain. He and his friends had a relationship that was different than that, they knew that they could only hope to accomplish this through God's power. He went to inform them of the king's demands so they could join together in prayer.

Time and again we see Daniel faced with difficult circumstances. Each time he had the choice to choose prayer or panic. While it's easy to assume that Daniel never questioned God's faithfulness, ability, or power, we know that even those who appear strong and confident can face insecurity and doubts when isolated and alone. When there is a strong community around them, even those with insecurity and doubts know where to turn.

Last week we saw how these four friends encouraged and supported one another in their faith. Now we see they also prayed together. They understood the power of having a God-centered community. Together they pleaded for God to be merciful, to reveal the dream and spare their lives.

> *"For where two or three gather in my name, there am I with them."*
>
> Matthew 18:20

Like Daniel, we too need a Godly community of friends we can trust to pray with us, provide encouragement, and remind us of God's faithfulness when times get tough. But we can't hope to establish these deep meaningful relationships during a crisis. They have to be intentionally nurtured in advance.

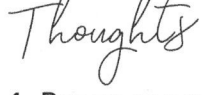

1. Prayer or panic - which one is your default when times get tough? Why is that your first response?

2. Evaluate your current friendships. Do you have a community or friend that you could ask to join in prayer, encouragement or support during a hard season? If not, getting involved in a serving group is one of the best ways to begin building community.

3. Write a prayer either thanking God for the Godly friendships in your life or asking Him to bring the right people into your life to build the community He longs for you to experience.

Context: Daniel praises God for answering their prayers by revealing the king's dream.

Have you ever had God answer your prayer in a miraculous way? Maybe finances were tight and you received the exact amount needed to pay a bill. Or someone you know received a diagnosis then learned there was no sign of disease at a follow up appointment.

Today we see that God miraculously answered Daniel and his friends by giving Daniel a vision of the king's dream! While you and I might have immediately run to tell King Nebuchadnezzar what we'd learned, Daniel had a different response.

First, Daniel immediately trusted God had answered their prayers. As soon as he received God's revelation, Daniel knew He had answered. There was no hesitation. He didn't wake his friends to get their opinion, wondering if he'd heard God correctly. He didn't consider if they should keep praying in case there was more to uncover, as though God was holding out on them. He knew without a doubt that this was God.

Next, Daniel praised God. Daniel was in the middle of a crisis. Time was running out and lives (including his own) depended on him describing and interpreting this dream. It would have been natural for him to drop everything to share what he'd learned with the king. But God always comes first to Daniel. He is his Lord, his source of strength and wisdom. For Daniel there's no other option. He has to first praise God for his wisdom, power, and answered prayers.

Not only would their lives be spared, when he interpreted the dream, but Daniel knew this would illustrate God's power to King Nebuchanezzar.

> *"In Him (Jesus) and through faith in Him we may approach God with freedom and confidence.*
>
> Ephesians 3:12

Sometimes we pray, but deep down wonder if God will really come through. We pray with hesitation. We devise our own back up plan just in case God doesn't answer. Sometimes when He answers our prayers, we're often quick to move on, barely acknowledging it was God who supplied our need, opened the door, provided direction and clarity, or like in Daniel's case, performed a miracle.

We are God's children. He loves us, forgives us, redeems us, and chooses us. He wants us to know that through Jesus, we can boldly bring our prayers to Him. And when He answers, may we pause to praise Him from a heart full of gratitude.

Thoughts

1. Consider your prayer life. Do you come to God with hesitation or confidence? Why?

2. How do you respond when God answers your prayers? Are you quick to move forward? Or do you pause to thank and praise God for what He's done?

3. Write a prayer asking God to help you trust Him more as you confidently bring your prayers to Him.

Context: Daniel interprets Nebuchadnezzar's dream.

God is such a mystery! From a cloud by day and fire by night[1] to a still small voice[2], to Jesus Himself[3] - the Bible is full of ways God reveals Himself to man. He also uses parables or stories, dreams and metaphors. In fact, Nebuchadnezzar's dream was actually a metaphor or symbol of something else, which is why he needed someone to translate it for him.

First, Daniel describes the dream. He intentionally says "we" (vs 36) as a way to credit his friends and spare their lives. Daniel described a large statue made of four different materials, each one representing an empire. The gold head represented the Babylonian empire, the silver chest and arms the Medo-Persian empire, the bronze torso and thighs the Greek empire. Finally, the iron and clay legs and feet represented the Roman empire. Daniel finishes by describing a rock that was cut from a mountain, but it wasn't cut by human hands. The rock represents God.

Then Daniel interprets what it all means. The Rock (God) will smash each part of the statue, defeating every earthly empire and establish His kingdom that will never be destroyed.

It would have been easy for Daniel and his friends to take credit for being able to accommodate the king's demand. However, Daniel was quick to sum up his explanation by giving all the credit and glory to God for showing the king the meaning of his dream.

The same holds true for us. When God is gracious to reveal Himself by answering our prayers - maybe by confirming a decision, providing healing, or restoring a broken relationship - we should be quick to publicly acknowledge Him for all He's done.

Thoughts

1. Why do you think God uses so many ways to reveal Himself to us? Which way(s) has he revealed Himself to you?

2. Think of a time when God answered your prayer. Did you publicly credit Him when given the opportunity? For example, when sharing a story of how things fell into place, are you comfortable sharing that it was God who made it happen? Why or why not?

3. Write a prayer asking God to help you become more mindful of how He's working in your life and have the courage to give Him all the glory.

---

[1] *Exodus 13:21*
[2] *1 Kings 19:12-13*
[3] *Colossians 1:15-16*

Context: King Nebuchadnezzar is awestruck by the miracle he just witnessed, promoting Daniel and his friends to higher positions of influence in Babylon.

Once again this week, we've seen Daniel and his friends' unwavering faith and commitment to God in the middle of an intense situation. And once again we've seen God move in mighty ways to provide wisdom, courage, and protection.

Today we see the impact of their faithfulness. King Nebuchadnezzar didn't believe in the One true God. As the Babylonian king, He worshiped a variety of gods. He depended on magicians and enchanters (today we call them psychics and fortune tellers) for spiritual guidance. We know their efforts fell short and Daniel, through God's power, was able to describe and translate the king's dream, giving all the glory to God. This provided an opening for God to make himself real, not only to Daniel and his friends, but to King Nebuchadnezzar too.

After Daniel successfully revealed the details of the dream, Nebuchadnezzar fell on the ground praising Daniel's God and had an offering presented as a way to honor Him. It's here that the king recognizes God "as the God of gods and Lord of kings."

The king also honored Daniel and his friends by promoting them yet again. This encounter between King Nebuchadnezzar and Daniel led to a relationship between the two men. In the days to come, we will see this relationship continue to impact the king as his admiration and respect for Daniel grew.

> *"For we are taking pains to do what is right, not only in the eyes of the Lord but also in the eyes of man."*
>
> 2 Corinthians 8:21

Daniel reminds us that our character matters. It matters to God and it matters to those around us. As we read about Daniel, we learn of his deep faith, but we also see that he is grateful, humble, respectful and gracious. He and his friends were men of integrity and character. Like Daniel, we have the opportunity to impact those around us - friends, family, neighbors, coworkers - by the way we live everyday. People notice when you have peace in the middle of life's storm or unexplainable joy or when you give credit to God for what He's doing in your life. Moments like these add up. They not only strengthen your own faith, they can be the open door for those around you to encounter Jesus.

Thoughts

1. If you follow Jesus, think about the person(s) who was instrumental in leading you to the Lord. What about their character drew you to them and ultimately made you trust their spiritual leadership?

2. Consider your own character. Do those around you know there's something different about you because of your relationship with Jesus? If not, what needs to change?

3. Write a prayer to God asking Him to reveal areas in your character that need to be more like Him.

GROUP STUDY GUIDE
Among Lions: WHEN PRESSURE'S ON
WEEK OF OCTOBER 22, 2023

Synopsis:
In Daniel 1, we saw Babylon's strategy to influence Daniel. In chapter 2, we see Daniel's strategy to influence Babylon. God was at work in and through Daniel because he didn't isolate, blend in, or water down. He was deeply involved in others' lives who were far from God, and he lived unapologetically for God. When the pressure's on, God wants to give us a solid foundation so we can make a difference for Him.

*Note the following correction:
Daniel and his friends were taken to Babylon in 605BC, during the first invasion in the first year of Nebuchadnezzar's reign. Nebuchadnezzar's dream was revealed and interpreted in 604BC, the second year of his reign (Daniel 2:1). Jeremiah 29 was written to exiles taken to Babylon in 597BC, nine years after Daniel and his friends were taken, not before.

WARM UP QUESTION:
What is the weirdest dream you've ever had?

DISCUSS:

Read Daniel 2:1-13 together out loud:

• What details stand out to you in these verses?

• What do these verses reveal about King Nebuchadnezzar?

• What do they reveal about the astrologers in his kingdom?

Read Daniel 2:14-30.

• What steps did Daniel take when he learned about the king's decree? Consider highlighting them or creating a list together

• If you were in his shoes, what would you probably do? • •
• Which of Daniel's actions would be hardest for you to do?

• What stands out to you in Daniel's words of praise in verses 20-23?

• Among the attributes of God he mentions, which one is most encouraging or comforting to you personally right now? Why?

Read Daniel 2:31-49.

• What observations, questions, or takeaways do you have about the dream and its interpretation? Talk through those together, and reference your sermon notes and Study Bible footnotes for insights on anything that is confusing.

RESPOND:
• As you reflect back on this story, are you more challenged by Daniel's side of the story or Nebuchadnezzar's? Why?

• What specifically is God challenging you to do or change as a result? Spend a few minutes sharing with each other what you sense God asking you to do this week and when you will do it.

• In your group prayer time, praise God for being in control, and pray that He would be a solid foundation in each of your lives as you live for Him this week.

*Encourage group members to read Daily Bible Reading on the church app or have it delivered to their inbox daily. Subscribe at **www.thecrossinglv.com/app**. Check in with your group to share thoughts about these throughout the week!*

LEADER NOTES: Access to weekly message, podcast, & notes at www.rightnowmedia.org

Among Lions: IN THE LINE OF FIRE

36

Context: Shadrach, Meshach and Abednego face a spiritual challenge without Daniel

Until now, our focus has been centered around Daniel's faith and relationship with King Nebuchadnezzar. This week, we take a deeper look at his three friends - Shadrach, Meshach, and Abednego.

We've learned that these three were incredible friends to Daniel, joining him in prayer and supporting him as he stood up to King Nebuchadnezzar. We also know that the king has promoted them to important positions within the empire. Now they're faced with their own life and death encounter with the king without Daniel's help. The Bible doesn't say where he is during the course of events. All we know is that he was not involved or mentioned.

They had to decide for themselves if they would remain faithful to their own commitment to God or bow down to the king. They couldn't rely on Daniel's faith to sustain them. They couldn't depend on his courage to make them brave enough to face the king. They couldn't count on him to be their spokesman. They had to decide whom they would serve.

> " But if serving the Lord seems undesirable to you, then choose for yourselves this day whom you will serve. But as for me and my household, we will serve the Lord." [1]
>
> Joshua 24:15

The same is true for each of us. Yes, it's important for us to have a healthy, Godly community to encourage and support one another. But we can't substitute someone else's faith for our own. Each of us will encounter a situation that requires us to make our faith our own. To decide if we're willing to stand up for God even when others around us chose not to. We can't rely solely on the faith of a parent, grandparent, mentor, pastor or friend to be our foundation. If it is, then we have to ask ourselves where our faith is really grounded - in God or someone else?

Thoughts

1. Think over your own walk with God. Have you had a time when you had to make your faith your own? What did you choose? Why did you make that choice?

2. It's important to have spiritual leaders in your life, but we have to be careful that we don't substitute their faith for our own. Consider your mentors. Are you ever tempted to rely on their faith instead of making your own decision to follow God completely?

3. Write a prayer asking God to give you courage as you learn to take ownership of your relationship with Jesus.

---

[1]*This verse has been condensed. The complete verse reads, "But if serving the Lord seems undesirable to you, then choose for yourselves this day whom you will serve, whether the gods your ancestors served beyond the Euphrates, or the gods of the Amorites, in whose land you are living. But as for me and my household, we will serve the Lord." Joshua 24:15 (NIV)*

Context: King Nebuchadnezzar builds a huge statue and demands everyone to bow down in worship.

The Bible doesn't say how much time has passed since Daniel revealed the king's dream to him and the king responded with praise and offerings to God, but it was enough for King Nebuchadnezzar to have a golden statue 90' high by 9' wide built for everyone to worship. Upon completion, he commanded that every one was to bow down and worship the statue or risk being thrown into a fiery furnace.

But wait. After his dream was translated, didn't King Nebuchadnezzar acknowledge Daniel's God as the "God of gods and Lord of kings"[2]? Yes he did. However, we see that acknowledgement of God's power doesn't always lead to a transformed heart.

Although the king praised God, his devotion was short-lived. He didn't begin to obey or honor God. He didn't stop worshiping other gods and idols. He didn't encourage others to follow God. The king's heart hadn't changed. Instead, he minimized God's power and holiness by adding Him to the list of gods and idols that he already worshiped.

Chances are you don't have a 90' statue you worship. But idols don't have to be that prominent to shift our focus and attention away from God. They can be subtle and even good things like a relationship, career, family, ministry or goal. Whatever is taking God's rightful first place in our lives, is an idol. The good news is that God is forgiving. He longs to be first in our lives and He offers us grace as we come to Him with a humble heart that is willing to change.

It's possible to know a lot about God and still not follow Him. Knowledge alone doesn't lead to salvation. There has to be an internal difference. In other words, it's not enough to declare God as Lord, as we've seen with King Nebuchadnezzar. There must also be a change of heart because everything else flows from it.

> *"If you declare with your mouth, "Jesus is Lord," and believe in your heart that God raised him from the dead, you will be saved.*
>
> **Romans 10:9**

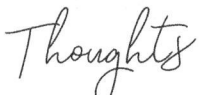

1. One of the values of The Crossing is that transformation is the expectation of every believer. How would you describe your transformation or change since following Jesus?

2. An idol by definition is an image or representation of god used as an object of worship. Examine your own heart. Is there anything that is currently distracting you from making God your first priority?

3. Write a prayer confessing anything that's taken God's place in your life. Invite Him to transform your heart as you make Him your first love.

---

²*Daniel 2:47*

Context: Shadrach, Meshach and Abednego risk their lives by taking a stand against the king's demand

Have you ever made excuses for your behavior even when you knew it contradicted what God wanted you to do? Maybe you cut corners at work to please a client. Or cheated on a test because you needed to pass the class. Or told a white lie to avoid an argument. I mean it's not that big of a deal, right? Other people do a lot worse. Besides, God understands, doesn't He?

Today we see how Shadrach, Meshach and Abednego were in a similar situation. Once again, King Nebuchadnezzar had implemented a decree with deadly consequences for anyone who refused to comply. As we learned yesterday, anyone who was unwilling to bow down to the newly constructed gold statue would face a fiery furnace.

Remember, after Daniel revealed the king's dream, he promoted the three friends to prominent government positions. Now as part of their job, they along with governors and officials from across the empire gathered to dedicate the golden statue. As the musicians began to play, signaling it was time for everyone to bow before the statue, Shadrach, Meshach and Abednego had a choice to make.

Put yourself in their shoes….or sandals. They've lived through the king's unpredictable rage before. They knew he didn't make empty threats. They understood Daniel wasn't there to advocate for them if things went wrong. It would have been easy for them to make excuses in order to save their lives. For example:

1. They could have decided to bow but not worship the statue in their hearts.

2. They could have decided to do it just this once so their lives would be spared, then ask God for forgiveness.
3. They could have decided God would understand because it's the king. They had to obey.
4. They could have decided they owed the king their loyalty for promoting them.
5. They could have decided they couldn't save their people if they were dead.

Any of these excuses would have been reasonable… to man. Cutting corners to find a way to please both God and man never works. Shadrach, Meshach and Abednego understood they had to be willing to follow God whatever it might cost them.

> "The Lord will keep you from all harm – He will watch over your life; the Lord will watch over your coming and going both now and for evermore"
>
> Psalm 121:7-8

Thoughts

1. Think about a time when you cut corners or compromised in order to please man or help yourself. How did you feel afterwards?

2. What excuses do you use when faced with the tension between saving yourself or pleasing God?

3. Write a prayer asking God to give you courage to choose to follow Him even when the consequences could be costly.

Context: Shadrach, Meshach and Abednego declare God's goodness even if He doesn't save them.

It's easy to trust that God is good when we see Him show up in mighty ways in our lives. But what about when He doesn't answer your prayers the way you'd hope? Are you still able to trust in God's goodness even then?

Shadrach, Meshach and Abednego saw God's faithfulness when He made a way for them to be set apart by not eating the king's food and again when He saved their lives by revealing the king's dream to Daniel. They knew He was able to do miraculous things. However, when they stood before the king to defy his command, they spoke with confidence in both God's ability to save them AND and in His sovereignty if He chose not to.

One of the most powerful yet humbling lines in the Bible comes from these three friends when they tell the king, "But even if He (God) doesn't (save us) we will not serve your gods or worship the image you have set up." What a bold and courageous response! King Nebuchadnezzar was furious. He ordered the furnace heated seven times hotter than usual and commanded some of the strongest soldiers in his army to tie them up and throw them into the blazing furnace.

At any point God could have intervened, preventing the trio from being thrown into the furnace - before they were bound, as they walked with the guards to the furnace, just before being thrown inside. But God chose not to. Why? Because God had a greater plan to illustrate His power and might.

> *"Do not fear, for I have redeemed you; I have summoned you by name; you are mine. When you pass through the waters, I will be with you; and when you pass through the rivers, they will not sweep over you. When you walk through the fire, you will not be burned; the flames will not set you ablaze. For I am the Lord your God, the Holy One of Israel, your Savior"*
>
> Isaiah 43:1b-3a

Maybe you're in a fire right now. Your faith is being challenged and you need God to show up. Yet, as much as you pray, it feels like He's not listening. Things continue to get worse and you're starting to lose hope. Jesus told us we would have troubles because we live in a sinful, broken world. Being a Christian doesn't mean we're exempt from pain and suffering. However, God also promised we would never go trials alone. And He is still good regardless of the outcome.

Thoughts

1. Shadrach, Meshach and Abednego believed God was good even if He allowed them to die in the fire. Are you able to trust in God's goodness even when He doesn't answer your prayers the way you hoped?

2. Think about a time in your life when you thought God should have intervened and He didn't. How did that impact your relationship with Him?

3. Write an honest prayer to God expressing your feelings towards Him about the situation you reflected on from question #2. Invite Him to heal any anger, brokenness or resentment you may have that is causing you to keep Him at a distance.

Context: Shadrach, Meshach and Abednego are miraculously saved from the fire.

Once again, the king witnessed God perform a miracle! Not only did He save Shadrach, Meshach and Abednego from the fire, but when he looked inside, King Nebuchadnezzar saw a fourth person among the flames! The Bible isn't specific on this person's identity. Maybe it was an angel, or a heavenly form of Jesus. Either way, God sent a companion to accompany these three faithful friends literally through the fire.

It says the king was so amazed at what he saw that he immediately called for the trio to come to him. Can you imagine? You just witnessed the fire's intensity kill the guards who threw the three friends into the flames, and now you're watching Shadrach, Meshach and Abednego walk out, completely unharmed. In fact, the Bible says they didn't even smell of smoke!

The king's response was almost identical to what he'd done after Daniel revealed his dream - he acknowledged God's power and established Him among Babylon's gods. This time he added a decree that anyone who spoke against this God would be killed.

Yesterday we saw that Shadrach, Meshach and Abednego were submitted to God's will even if He didn't save them. However, they still believed God was able to save them. Elevation Worship has a song called *More Than Able* that includes the questions, "How did I start to believe You weren't sufficient for me? Why do I talk myself out of seeing miracles?" What powerful questions. So often we believe that God is able, but we're content to consistently operate with a mustard-seed size faith, while praying with the scarcity mentality of "God can, but He probably won't." This must break His heart.

> "Now to him who is able to do immeasurably more than all we ask or imagine, according to his power that is at work within us."
>
> Ephesians 3:20

If we believe the Bible when it says that God is the same yesterday, today, and forever [3], then we have to believe that He is the same miracle-working God for us that He was for Shadrach, Meshach and Abednego. God loves His children beyond measure. He longs to walk with us through life's fires to provide help, encouragement, and support along the way. He's not only *able* to deliver us, He *longs* to and is *waiting for us* to invite Him to do so, with a heart of expectation.

Thoughts

1. Consider your own expectations of God. Do you believe He is able AND willing to deliver you? Or do you pray with a scarcity mindset?

2. Do you believe God still does miracles today? If not, like the song asks, "Why have you talked yourself out of seeing miracles?"

3. Write a prayer asking God to increase your faith and trust that He is not only able but willing to deliver you from the challenges and struggles you're going through.

---

[3] Hebrews 13:8

GROUP STUDY GUIDE
Among Lions: IN THE LINE OF FIRE
WEEK OF OCTOBER 29, 2023

Synopsis:
When Daniel's friends were told to bow down to a golden idol, they were courageous in their convictions. As a result, they were thrown into a fiery furnace. We all face our own furnaces that ultimately reveal who we are and who we're becoming. When we go into the heat, we're not alone. We can trust God to refine us to become more like Him.

WARM UP QUESTION:
Where is the hottest place you've ever been, and what was it like?

DISCUSS:

Read Daniel 3:1-18 together out loud:

• Based on what you've just read, what do you think about King Nebuchadnezzar? What do you think about the astrologers who came forward (verses 8-12)?

• What stands out to you in the response of Shadrach, Meshach, and Abednego in verses 16-18?

• What modern-day situations can you think of that put pressure on followers of Jesus to "bow down" to something or someone other than God?

Read Daniel 3:19-30.

• If you were in the shoes of Shadrach, Meshach, and Abednego, what would you be thinking as the furnace is being prepared for you?

• How does the appearance of the fourth man encourage you personally or challenge what you think about God? Is there a time in your life when you've been in a "fiery furnace" and felt or experienced God's presence? Explain.

• What areas of your life are under more heat than others

right now? How does the story in this passage challenge or encourage you?

• What steps could you take this week to build your faith in preparation for the "furnace" (or in the midst of it)?

RESPOND:
• What specific step do you think God is prompting you to do first? When will you do it?

• Spend a few minutes praying together. Pray for anyone in your group walking through a "furnace" right now, and pray for each person to carve out time this week to build their faith in God's presence.

Encourage group members to read Daily Bible Reading on the church app or have it delivered to their inbox daily. Subscribe at **www.thecrossinglv.com/app**. *Check in with your group to share thoughts about these throughout the week!*

LEADER NOTES: Access to weekly message, podcast, & notes at www.rightnowmedia.org

Among Lions: WRITING ON THE WALL

Context: Several years later, Daniel interprets another dream for King Nebuchadnezzar.

This week, our focus shifts back to Daniel and King Nebuchadnezzar. It's been several years since Daniel volunteered to interpret the king's dream. Now he finds himself in a very similar situation. King Nebuchadnezzar has had another mysterious dream. Based on his previous success, you might think the king immediately summoned Daniel to interrupt this new dream. Instead, the king fell back into old habits, calling on his magicians again. When they were unable to provide an explanation, he remembered Daniel.

God allowed Daniel to understand the dream. For the first time, we read that Daniel was "greatly perplexed and his thoughts terrified him."[1] God revealed that the king, like the mighty tree in his dream, had grown in power and success. But his success wouldn't last. He would be "cut down," and forced to live like a wild animal in the wilderness. No wonder Daniel was afraid! He knew this message predicted the fall of King Nebuchadnezzar. BUT - God gave the king one more chance - a way to avoid destruction - confess his sin, accept God as Lord (not just another god), and be compassionate. In fact, God gave him a year to decide to make Him the Lord of his life, but his pride continued to stand in the way.

> *"First pride, then the crash. The bigger the ego, the harder the fall."*
>
> Proverbs 16:1(MSG)

Many of us fall into the same cycle. When life is hard, we desperately seek God for help. But when life is going well, we often forget about our daily dependence on Him and reclaim control of our lives. Pride goes even further. It's a condition of the heart that believes we don't really need God. God and pride can't coexist. As we will see tomorrow, God will discipline us when necessary.

Thoughts

1. Consider your current relationship with God. Are you daily depending on Him or are you in control?

2. Pride is hard for us to see in ourselves, but easy to spot in others. Think of someone in your life that you can receive honest feedback from. Allow them permission to speak into your life, helping you identify where pride may be a blindspot for you.

3. Write a prayer to God, confessing the pride in your heart. Ask Him for forgiveness as you learn to humbly make Him Lord of your life.

---

[1] Daniel 5:19

Context: King Nebuchadenzzar's dream is fulfilled. He becomes insane for a period of time, but God provides a path to redemption

What comes to mind when you hear the word discipline? Punishment? Consequences? Anger? Disappointment?

Whether a child by a parent, student by a teacher, employee by a boss - No one likes to be disciplined. It can be humiliating, embarrassing, and at times, even painful. God uses discipline to help us. That might sound harsh. Isn't there a more kind, gentle and loving way to teach us to depend on Him? Yes. But as we've seen with King Nebuchadnezzar, sometimes our stubbornness and pride prevent that from being effective.

Daniel warned the king God's discipline could be avoided but he didn't listen. As promised, God gave the king a year to submit to his authority, but he refused. He attributed Babylon's power, wealth and might to his own human ability as king, taking all the glory for himself. His stubbornness forced God to discipline him. The king became insane. He lived in the wilderness, eating grass like cattle. His hair grew long like eagle feathers and his nails became like claws. That's a pretty drastic way to get someone's attention. But God is willing to do drastic things to draw us back to Himself.

God desired a relationship with King Nebuchadnezzar. He longed for him to humble himself and allow God to be Lord of his life, so he provided a pathway for forgiveness and redemption. Ironically, it was the same pathway as before - humble confession + acknowledgement of God as Lord.

> *"The Lord is not slow in keeping his promise, as some understand slowness. Instead he is patient with you, not wanting anyone to perish, but everyone to come to repentance."*

Ephesians 3:20

God doesn't discipline us because He's mad at us. God is a loving Father who patiently waits for us. He doesn't want anyone to miss out on eternity with Him. He deeply desires a relationship with us. So much so, that He's willing to do what it takes to get our attention and draw our hearts to Him.

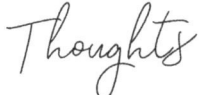

1. Consider a time when you were disciplined. Looking back, can you see how God might have been using that experience to refine your character?

2. Have you ever felt too ashamed or unworthy to receive God's forgiveness and redemption? Take some time today to allow the truth that God's love covers every sin to encourage and comfort you.

3. Write a prayer asking God to help you identify areas of your heart and character that need to submit to His authority, and the humility to let Him transform those places.

4. If you've never invited God to be the Lord of your life and are ready to do so, let us help you take that next step. Go to: **thecrossinglv.com/decision**, or use the QR code below.

Context: After the death of Nebuchadnezzar, several men ruled Babylon. Belshazzar, the current king, holds a large banquet for a thousand of his nobles when a mysterious writing appears on the wall.

It's been several years since King Nebuchadnezzar's death. His descendant, King Belshazzar, is the new ruler of Babylon. Like Nebuchadnezzar, he too chose to disregard God and in turn trust magicians and fortune tellers. In fact, that's who he initially calls on to translate a mysterious message that appeared on the wall during a lavish banquet.

While the king entertained one thousand of his nobles, he demanded that the gold and silver goblets that King Nebuchadnezzar had taken from the temple in Jerusalem during his siege, be brought in so he and his guests could use them. We'll look at this in greater detail tomorrow. As the party continues, King Belshazzar notices a finger writing on the wall! LIke Nebuchadnezzar, he summoned his magicians to provide an explanation. As before, they were unable to reveal the meaning. It's then that the queen reminds Belshazzar about Daniel. He's called to the palace and once again God allows him to interpret the meaning of the writing on the wall - MENE MENE - TEKEL - PARSIN, which predicted the king's fall from power.

Yesterday we saw that God gave Nebuchadnezzar opportunities to submit to His authority and make Him the Lord of his life, but his heart was unwilling. Now we see his descendant acted the same way.

History has a way of repeating itself, especially within families. Eventually, we start making excuses like "our family's always been this way" in an attempt to minimize or excuse our behavior. Nebuchadnezzar ruled from a heart of arrogance and pride. Those same characteristics had been passed down and now Belshazzar ruled Babylon in the same way.

It's easy to cast blame. Self reflection is much harder. Honestly assessing to see where our own actions, choices, character, and integrity might be lacking requires humility. Maybe your family history is tarnished, but that doesn't mean you have to follow their footsteps. God is a God of new beginnings! He gave His son Jesus to set the captives free...to set you free! By His grace, He is able to break the chains of your past.

> "So if the Son sets you free, you will be free indeed."
>
> John 8:36

Thoughts

1. Think back over your own family. Where do you see a history of disobedience that's been passed down and now excused? (ie: finances, pride, adultery, fear, addiction)

2. Consider your own life. Where do you feel bound to the past? What would it take for you to trust God to break the chains and set you free?

3. Write a prayer asking God to help you see any blindspots you may have regarding your own heart. Then invite Him to bring freedom to those areas.

Context: King Belshaazar used gold and silver goblets taken from God's temple in Jerusalem to toast the gods of Babylon.

King Belshaazar held an elaborate party for one thousand of his nobles. During the festivities, he called for the gold and silver goblets that King Nebuchadnezzar had taken from God's temple in Jerusalem, to be brought in so everyone could toast to the gods of gold, silver, bronze, iron, stone and wood.[2]

They're just cups. What's the big deal? But to God they weren't simply insignificant items that had been stolen. They were a physical representation of God's holiness and favor. The king was making a mockery of the God they represented. Even as the toast was happening, the writing on the wall began to appear warning of the impending consequences.

God gives us the same warning. In Galatians 6:7, we're reminded that God will not be mocked. What a person sows they will reap. In other words, we can't dishonor or disrespect God and not expect consequences.

Perhaps you're thinking, "I would never mock or dishonor God!" We'd like to think that we'd never use God or abuse what God's given us for our own benefit. And still, it happens all the time.

> "Create in me a pure heart, O God, and renew a steadfast spirit within me."
>
> Psalms 51:10

God has given each of us gifts, talents, and resources for us to use for His glory. It's up to us to examine our own motives and how we're using what He's so graciously provided. We often think of worship as singing songs on Sunday morning. But another way to honor Him is by using what God has blessed us with to bring Him honor & glory.

Thoughts

1. Think about the abilities, talents and resources God's given you. How have you used them for your own glory? How can you begin to shift the focus and start using them as a way to worship God?

2. Consider your own motives. Are there areas of your life that you've disrespected or dishonored God with your words or actions?

3. Write a prayer asking God to help you see where you might be operating from selfish motives. Confess that to Him and invite Him to create a clean heart in you today.

---

[2] Daniel 5:4

Context: Nebuchadnezzar's vision of a statue with silver arms and chest is fulfilled.

> "For the wages of sin is death, but the gift of God is eternal life in Christ Jesus our Lord."
>
> **Romans 6:23**

In Daniel 2, we learned that God predicted that Babylon would be taken over by other empires. This prediction was made through Nebuchadnezzar's dream about a statue made of different materials. Decades later, we see this prediction, or prophecy, finally happen.

After being reminded of Daniel's ability to interpret dreams, King Belshazzar brought him to his banquet to translate the mysterious writing on the wall. Daniel explained that the message said that the king's days as ruler were coming to an end and his kingdom would be divided between the Medes and the Persians.[3]

That very same night, King Darius the Mede, invaded Babylon, killing King Belshazzar and taking over the kingdom.

Prophecy or predictions are found throughout the Bible, not just in the book of Daniel. Isaiah, Jeremiah, Ezekiel, and Revelation have details that point to future events, some of which have already happened. For example Isaiah foretold Jesus' birth 700 years before it occurred.[4] Other prophecies, like those in the book of Revelations, give insight of things to come.

The idea of predicting the future can both intrigue and frighten us. It can tempt us to search for answers to Biblical questions. God uses prophecy to speak, guide and warn us. However, God doesn't give us vague details in the hopes that we will put the pieces of a divine puzzle together. Rather, we can have hope in the knowledge that while we don't understand the how, when, where and why, God does. He is in control and we can trust Him with the unknown.

> *"But about that day or hour no one knows, not even the angels in heaven or the Son of Man."*
>
> **Matthew 24:36**

1. When you read through the Biblical prophecy, do you find yourself more intrigued or fearful?

2. Do you struggle to trust God with the unknown? Are you ever tempted to search for answers to God's mysteries instead of trusting He's in control?

3. Write a prayer asking God to help you trust Him when you don't understand or become fearful of what you don't understand.

---

³*Daniel 5:26-28*
⁴*Isaiah 9:6-7*

GROUP STUDY GUIDE
Among Lions: WRITING ON THE WALL
WEEK OF NOVEMBER 5, 2023

Synopsis:
Pride is a blind spot that we often don't recognize in ourselves until it's too late. In Daniel 4-5, God confronts the pride of two powerful kings. It's a story about how He ultimately brought down the Babylonian Empire, but it also shows how He deals with prideful, rebellious people in all times and places. God will always have the final word. Our hope isn't in our circumstances. It's in Him.

WARM UP QUESTION:
What personal accomplishment are you most proud of, and why?

DISCUSS:
In Daniel 4, Nebuchadnezzar has a dream about a large, strong tree that gets cut down. Daniel interprets it, explaining that Nebuchadnezzar is the tree and that he will go from being powerful to being a madman. See what happens one year later by having someone read Daniel 4:28-37 out loud.

• What actions and phrases stand out to you in verses 28-30? How do they point to Nebuchadnezzar's pride?

• What do the remaining verses show you about: (1) the consequences of pride, and (2) where we're supposed to focus our affection instead?

A few generations later, another king is ruling in Babylon. Read his story in Daniel 5 together, splitting the chapter between 3-5 different group members if helpful.

• What similarities do you see between Belshazzar and his ancestor Nebuchadnezzar? What differences do you see? If helpful, create columned lists with what you observe.

- Looking at verses 1-9, what things did Belshazzar "numb out" with? Do you turn to similar things in your own life? If not, what do you "numb out" with instead?

- What's your gut reaction to the message that was written on the wall and how quickly it was fulfilled (verses 25-31)?

- God uses a lot of different things to get our attention, even drawing on a wall with the "finger of God" if necessary. What are some different ways He has been speaking to you lately? Is there a repeating theme in what He's saying? Explain.

- Looking back at Belshazzar's and Nebuchadnezzar's stories, what one thing convicts you the most? How does it apply to your personal life?

RESPOND:
- Spend a few minutes in quiet reflection, asking God to show you what your personal next step is. Then have each person share their goal for the week and when they'll do it.

- Pray for each other to recognize the traps of pride or "numbing out" in your own lives and for courage to take the next step God is asking of you.

*Encourage group members to read Daily Bible Reading on the church app or have it delivered to their inbox daily. Subscribe at **www.thecrossinglv.com/app**. Check in with your group to share thoughts about these throughout the week!*

LEADER NOTES: Access to weekly message, podcast, & notes at www.rightnowmedia.org

Among Lions:
AMONG LIONS

Context: Daniel is an old man still living in Babylon which is now ruled by King Darius.

Have you ever felt like your age hindered you? Maybe you've felt too young to lead or have an impact on those around you. Or maybe you've felt too old, questioning if your best years are behind you or does God still have a purpose for your life. As we've seen throughout the life of Daniel, God *can and does* use us at any age. In chapter 1, we saw a young Daniel's impact on King Nebuchadnezzar as he interpreted dreams. Now we read that even into his eighties, he continued to have an influence on those around him.

Last week we learned that King Darius took over Babylon after defeating King Belshazzar. Like the kings before him, Darius appointed Daniel to a powerful position in the kingdom. What made Daniel so influential that one king after another found favor and elevated him? Was he really that smart? Did he make himself indispensable? Did he manipulate and scheme his way to the top? No. While Daniel was gifted, he recognized that everything he had - his talent, protection, positions - all came from God. He performed his daily tasks as though he was doing them for God and not a king. Daniel wasn't motivated by a king's validation or praise. His motives were simply to please God in all things.

> "So whether you eat or drink or whatever you do, do it all for the glory of God.
>
> 1 Corinthians 10:31

Daniel didn't desire popularity or strive to prove his worth. Yes, God used him to do significant things. But over the span of a lifetime, those major events were very few. The majority of his life was spent in faithful service to God and others. Daniel, like us, was called to a life of integrity and faithfulness. By living each day from a place of humility, gratitude, and dependency, God was able to use Daniel for HIS purpose.

Everyone has a desire to know they matter and have a purpose. For many of us, that desire leads to frustration so we create our own destiny, while others become overwhelmed and defeated by the process. Maybe you're afraid of missing your purpose or discouraged believing that your purpose was wrapped up in the past. The truth is our purpose isn't a mystery to be solved. It's for each of us to live a life faithfully dedicated to God, bringing honor and glory to Him in everything we do.

Thoughts

1. Think back over your life. Have you ever felt too young or too old to be used by God? How did that season impact your relationship with God?

2. Consider your motives. Do you feel like you have to prove or strive to prove your worth? What would it look like for you to surrender your ideal purpose to be faithful right where He's placed you?

3. Write a prayer asking God to help you stay faithfully consistent as you keep Him at the center of everything you do.

Context: Daniel's coworkers conspire against him.

Have you ever had someone who was jealous of you? Maybe a friend who tried to sabotage a relationship or a coworker who held you back by taking credit for your work and ideas.

Yesterday we saw that Daniel's faithfulness, integrity and consistency made him a favorite among the kings. It also caused Daniel to make some enemies. Daniel's devotion to God ultimately set him apart. His work ethnic didn't depend on who the leader was at the time, if he liked them, or if he agreed with their policies. Daniel served one God and it was out of his love and devotion to Him, that he was able to serve each king well. However, this didn't make him popular with other Babylonian leaders.

Daniel was up against jealous men who envied his achievements and advantages. When they couldn't find fault in his character, they devised a plan to attack his faith. Daniel had a reputation of unwavering devotion to God throughout his life. Now his coworkers were using his faithfulness against him.

Like Daniel, our purest motives can come under attack when confronted by jealous people. On the other hand, we can be the one consumed with jealousy, unwilling to share what we have with others so we can get ahead. Our envy leads to discontentment. We see social media highlights of someone's life and wish we had their success, friends, money, title, house or vacation.

> "I am not saying this because I am in need, for I have learned to be content whatever the circumstances. I know what it is to be in need, and I know what it is to have plenty. I have learned the secret of being content in any and every situation, whether well fed or hungry, whether living in plenty or in want. I can do all this through him who gives me strength.
>
> Philippians 4:11-13

Daniel learned early in his life to be content whether a prisoner in exile or a chief administrator to the king. Those things didn't define him so they were of little value to him. Lifewise, when others were jealous of him and tried to tear him down, Daniel was unmoved because his confidence was in God alone.

Thoughts

1. Consider your own heart, is there anything you're jealousy protecting? What would it look like for you to surrender your selfishness and/or envy?

2. Examine your relationships. Is there anyone who's hurt you out of their own jealousy that you need to forgive?

3. Write a prayer asking for God to reveal and forgive any jealousy or discontentment you might have in your heart.

Context: Daniel continues praying three times a day despite King Darius' law forbidding any type of worship to anything or anyone other than himself.

Relationships take time, effort and intentionality to grow. Our relationship with God is no different. We can't expect to have a strong relationship with Him without intentionally and consistently showing up.

Daniel understood this. Over and over we've seen how his character was a direct reflection of his relationship with God. Daniel made God a priority by spending time with Him daily in prayer. He didn't wait until bad things happened to reach out to God. He stayed constantly connected to Him. In fact, after Daniel knew a law had been passed that forbid worship to anything other than the king, Daniel went to his upper room, knelt on his knees, gave thanks, and prayed.[1]

For many of us, prayer can be intimidating. We're not sure what to say or do so we avoid it. Prayer is simply a conversation with God, a time for you to honestly share what's on your heart with Him. Prayer invites us to be vulnerable with God, trusting Him with our fears, anxiety, emotions, and needs. It's also a time for us to be still so we can learn to listen to God's voice.

Prayer is also an opportunity to praise God for who He is and thank Him for what He's done. Daniel illustrated this multiple times when he gave God the glory for providing and protecting him.

> *"Do not be anxious about anything, but in every situation, by prayer and petition, with thanksgiving, present your requests to God. And the peace of God, which transcends all understanding, will guard your hearts and your minds in Christ Jesus."*
>
> **Philippians 4:6-7**

Like Daniel, we too can strengthen our relationship with God through daily prayer. If you're interested in deepening your relationship with God but are unsure where or how to begin, Rooted is a great place to start. It's a 10-week discipleship journey that explores how to invite God into your daily routine through things such as Bible reading, prayer, worship, and serving others. Although God desperately wants to spend time with you and grow your relationship, He will never force His way into your life. Instead He patiently waits to be invited.

Thoughts

1. Think about your daily routine. Do you currently prioritize time with God? If not, what needs to shift so you can begin to intentionally grow your relationship with Him?

2. Does prayer intimidate you? Or are you comfortable being honest and vulnerable with God?

3. Write a prayer praising God for who He is, thanking Him for what He's done in your life, and sharing any fear or need you have.

4. If you'd like to talk to someone about pursuing a deeper relationship with God, send an email to: **connect@thecrossinglv.com**

---

[1] *Daniel 6:10*

Context: Daniel is condemned to the lions' den.

King Darius didn't realize he and Daniel were being set up by the other jealous leaders until it was too late. His law had been signed and according to the Medes and Persians, the kingdom that ruled Babylon, once a law was enacted it couldn't be repealed, not even by the king. King Darius cared about Daniel and felt a deep sense of regret when he discovered he was to be killed. He couldn't eat or sleep. He spent the whole day trying to find a way to save Daniel. When his efforts failed, he had to follow through with his decree and send Daniel to the lion's den. Regret turned into guilt as the situation replayed over and over in his mind.

Have you been there? You long to make things right, but can't take back the words spoken in anger during an argument or undo the actions that hurt those you love. You don't know how to let go of the guilt and regret so you internalize it. Eventually shame sets in and you feel unworthy of forgiveness from them and God.

Maybe you're like Daniel and someone close to you betrayed your trust or hurt you deeply. You know they're sorry and wish they could take back what's been done, but the pain is too deep for you to get past by yourself.

> *"Be kind and compassionate to one another, forgiving each other, just as in Christ God forgave you."*
>
> **Ephesians 4:32**

In our own strength we can't move forward. But God always provides a way back to Himself, and if we're willing to each other. Forgiveness doesn't excuse behavior or consequences. It doesn't eliminate responsibility, but it does invite freedom from the anger and hurt, allowing space for healing to begin.

> *"If we confess our sins, he is faithful and just and will forgive us our sins and purify us from all unrighteousness."*
>
> 1 John 1:9

God doesn't expect us to carry the weight of our own guilt, shame and regrets as punishment. He doesn't determine your worth based on what you've done. He loves us too much - He loves you too much - to do that! In fact, that's why He sent Jesus. His blood covers every sin. There's nothing too bad that He's not able to forgive. All God requires is that we confess our sins and accept His gift of forgiveness.

1. Think about a time when you did or said something you regretted. Did your regret turn into shame? What needs to happen for you to accept God's forgiveness?

2. Consider a time when someone hurt you. How did your relationship with God impact your ability to offer forgiveness?

3. Write a prayer asking God to help you let go of regret, so that you can forgive yourself and others.

If you want to learn more about God's love and forgiveness, go to: **thecrossinglv.com/decision**, or use the QR code below.

Context: God saves Daniel from the lion's den. King Darius sentences the administrators to death instead.

Early the next morning, King Darius ran to the lion's den to check on Daniel. The king was amazed to find him alive without even a scratch. He immediately ordered that Daniel be pulled out of the den and the men who conspired against him thrown in along with their entire families.

While Daniel's life was marked by his faithfulness and devotion to God, God was equally devoted to Daniel. Time and again, we've seen God provide, protect and save Daniel.

Sometimes we read Bible stories like this and wonder if God still does miracles, and if so, would He do them for us? The same God who provided, protected, and saved Daniel is the same God who is alive and active in our lives. Sometimes we forget about what God's done for us. We take Him for granted or attribute what He's done to our own abilities. But the truth is God is just as mighty to save us as He was to save Daniel! We don't have to figure out the details, fix things ourselves, or work harder. Like Daniel, we simply need to be faithful and devoted to our God who loves us more than we can imagine.

> "The Lord your God is with you, the Mighty Warrior who saves. He will take great delight in you;
>
> Zephaniah 3:17a

After Daniel was pulled from the den, notice what he didn't do. He didn't tell the king who was responsible for this situation. He didn't try to get even. The Bible doesn't even suggest that Daniel was angry! Didn't Daniel care that these men had tried to kill him? Of course he did. But he didn't waste his energy on revenge. He trusted God to save him and he trusted God to bring judgment in His time.

> "Do not take revenge, my dear friends, but leave room for God's wrath, for it is written: "It is mine to avenge; I will repay,"says the Lord. On the contrary: "If your enemy is hungry, feed him; if he is thirsty, give him something to drink. In doing this, you will heap burning coals on his head." Do not be overcome by evil, but overcome evil with good."
>
> **Romans 12:19-21**

That's a hard one isn't it? We see injustice happen and feel like God doesn't care when He doesn't intervene in the way we think He should. We take it into our own hands to get even when we feel like God is taking too long to distribute judgment. Spiritual maturity comes when we are not only able to trust God with what we can see but with what we can't. Daniel understood that to completely trust God meant just that... completely trusting Him with the good and bad, the seen and unseen.

Thoughts

1. Do you think God can/will save you? Where have you seen God provide, protect or save you throughout your life?

2. If you're honest with yourself, do you completely trust God to deliver judgment in His time or do you feel compelled to take control?

3. Write a prayer inviting God to help you let go of control as you learn to fully trust Him.

GROUP STUDY GUIDE
Among Lions: AMONG LIONS
WEEK OF NOVEMBER 12, 2023

Synopsis:
Daniel's experience in the lions' den was his final demonstration of how to live for God within a godless culture. It was a result of small, daily acts behind closed doors when no one was looking. Daniel didn't suddenly muster up the courage to face a group of hungry lions. His character was built by the habits he formed over decades. Building his muscles of faith equipped him to be among lions.

WARM UP QUESTION:
What's the most dangerous animal encounter you've experienced or witnessed?

DISCUSS:

Read Daniel 6:1-9 together out loud:

• What do you notice about the environment and people surrounding Daniel in these verses? Are there any parallels to environments or people surrounding you?

• What stands out to you about Daniel's reputation? Do you find it easy or hard to distinguish yourself in this way? Explain.

Read Daniel 6:10-28 together out loud:

• If you were in Daniel's shoes, would you respond the same way he did in verse 10? Why or why not?

• What do you think the exchange between Darius and Daniel in verses 19-23 reveals about each of them? What else stands out to you in this exchange?

• Outside of closing the lions' mouths, where else do you see God at work in this passage?

• How do these observations encourage or challenge you today?

• As you look at this pinnacle of Daniel's legacy, what traits or actions impress you most? When you reach the end of your own life, what do you hope will be part of your personal legacy?

• In order for that to happen, what do you need to implement or change in your daily life right now?

RESPOND:
• Spend a few minutes allowing group members to quietly reflect on what their next step needs to be. Then share with each other what you'll do and when you'll do it.

• In your prayer time, consider assigning prayer partners who will pray for each other during group time but also throughout the week. Pray for hearts that are devoted to God at all ages and stages and for commitment to build daily rhythms that form godly character.

*Encourage group members to read Daily Bible Reading on the church app or have it delivered to their inbox daily. Subscribe at **www.thecrossinglv.com/app**. Check in with your group to share thoughts about these throughout the week!*

LEADER NOTES: Access to weekly message, podcast, & notes at www.rightnowmedia.org

Among Lions: ANCIENT OF DAYS

Context: Daniel has a vision of his own.

Throughout this series, we've seen God give Daniel the ability to reveal dreams and interpret messages for others. This week, we'll take a look at one of Daniel's own dreams.

As the chapter begins, we read that this dream occurred during the reign of Belshazzar, the king we learned about in chapter 5 who had Daniel interpret the writing on the wall. Knowing that Daniel had experience revealing mysteries, we might assume that he felt confident in his abilities, especially when we learn that this chapter is almost a mirror image of the dream that Daniel interpreted for King Nebuchadnezzar in chapter 2. In that dream, God revealed the fall of four earthly empires by using the image of a statue built from different materials and the rise of God's eternal kingdom that will be forever. This time, God reveals the same message by using the image of four beasts instead of a statue. God also provides more details to the eternal kingdom He is going to establish.

Each time Daniel had a vision or was called on to interpret one, he relied on God for help. This time was no different. Although Daniel had already interpreted the first dream, we learn he relies on an angel within his own dream to help him understand what he's seeing.

> "For my thoughts are not your thoughts, neither are your ways my ways," declares the Lord. "As the heavens are higher than the earth, so are my ways higher than your ways and my thoughts than your thoughts.
>
> Isaiah 55:8-9

As we grow in understanding, experience and success, it's easy to rely on our own abilities. And when things become unexplainable, we dismiss them as though they aren't from God. As we'll see this week, God's ways, timing, mysteries and methods are not like ours. They might even seem scary or crazy to us at times. But like Daniel, we can be encouraged even by the things we can't comprehend because God's already told us how things end, with Him on the throne.

1. Examine your own abilities. Which ones are you tempted to believe are due to your hard work, experience or success?

2. How do you feel when you are unable to understand what God is doing? Are you able to have peace knowing He's in control, or does the uncertainty cause you to be anxious or fearful?

3. Write a prayer asking God to help you let go of the things you don't fully comprehend and learn to trust Him.

Context: Daniel describes the four beasts in his dream.

Have you ever had a dream that stuck with you long after you woke up? Maybe you felt scared or anxious as you tried to make sense of it. Or maybe it was just too crazy to even put into words. That's exactly where Daniel finds himself.

In his dream, he sees four beasts unlike any beast or animal on earth. Daniel uses the word "like" over and over again to describe what he saw because the images were indescribable. First he describes a beast that was "like" a lion with wings "like" an eagle. The wings get torn off and the lion stands on two legs. The second beast was "like" a bear with three ribs in its mouth. The third beast was "like" a leopard with four heads and four wings on its back. The final beast Daniel saw was different than anything he'd ever seen. He's only able to describe it as terrifying, frightening, and very powerful with iron teeth and ten horns.

As Daniel tries to record his dream, he discovers that the things of heaven push our earthly language to its breaking point.

Many of us struggle to accept this. As humans, we want to understand the majesty and complexity of God. We try to confine God to a box that our minds can understand and explain. But there is no way our limited human knowledge can fully comprehend or explain an infinite God. His mysteries are far too great.

> "Can you fathom the mysteries of God? Can you probe the limits of the Almighty? They are higher than the heavens above—what can you do? They are deeper than the depths below—what can you know? Their measure is longer than the earth and wider than the sea."
>
> Job 11:7-9

Maybe you find yourself at a loss for words when you try to describe what God's done for you. You hesitate to share your story because you don't have the language to adequately illustrate the extreme love, forgiveness and healing He's brought to your life. Even the mysteries God allows us to experience can leave us speechless. Daniel did his best to find the words to describe the indescribable

Thoughts

1. What was the most unexplainable thing you've ever experienced?

2. When you consider God's mysteries, do you struggle to accept the things you can't explain or don't understand? What would it look like for you to trust God with the unexplainable?

3. Write a prayer asking Jesus to rebuke demons and evil from your home.

> **Context:** Daniel continues to describe his dream by introducing us to The Ancient of Days.

Have you ever been completely distracted by something, just to find out later that wasn't the most important piece of the puzzle or story? Maybe it was a character in a book or movie that you were fixated on just to discover they weren't as important as you thought. With the bizarre descriptions of the beasts, it might be easy to miss the most important part of what God is trying to tell Daniel and us.

Daniel's focus shifts from the four ferocious beasts to a new character he calls The Ancient of Days, which is God Himself. This is the only time in the Bible God is referred to by this name. Daniel specifically uses it to describe the eternal nature of God who has no beginning or end.

> "I am the Alpha and the Omega," says the Lord God, "who is, and who was, and who is to come, the Almighty."
>
> **Revelations 1:8**

Eternal and infinite are difficult concepts for us to understand. Not only is God eternal, but so is everything about Him - His wisdom, love, power and authority. Nothing has ever happened outside of God's will or knowledge nor will it in the future.

Daniel also described the Son of Man who comes into the presence of the Ancient of Days and is given all authority, glory and power. He goes on to learn that the Son of Man will be worshiped by everyone on earth. The Son of Man is Jesus. In fact, Jesus refers to himself this way in the New Testament.

> *"For even the Son of Man did not come to be served, but to serve, and to give his life as a ransom for many."*
>
> Mark 10:45

There were centuries between the time that Daniel had his dream and God sent Jesus to earth to bring salvation. Even during the gap we see that God was always in control. There was no need for man to worry then just like there's no need for us to be worried by the world today. We don't need to be distracted by the things happening around us. Instead, we can focus on the One who holds tomorrow in His hands, and trust that He is in control.

1. What is going on in your life that causes you to get easily distracted?

2. Do you find comfort and peace from knowing that God is eternal? Why or why not?

3. Write an honest prayer expressing how you feel about God's everlasting love for you.

Context: Daniel is troubled and confused by his dream and asks an angel for help.

What do you do when you don't understand something? Some people are intrigued and continue searching for information that leads to defined answers. Others become disinterested because it requires too much work. Still others find themselves overwhelmed and decide to give up.

We're a little more than half way through Daniel's dream and like most of us, he is having a hard time understanding what he sees. The images are troubling and disturbing. What did Daniel do? Did he chalk it up to a crazy dream? No. Did he try to use his own limited knowledge to explain the unexplainable? No. He asked for help.

Daniel writes that he saw a multitude of angels around God's throne.[1] He approached one of them and simply asked what all this meant. Tomorrow we'll discover what the angel revealed.

Sometimes we read a verse or passage in the Bible and find ourselves confused by its meaning, but we're not sure what to do next. It's hard to find an explanation if you're unsure where to look. We allow our lack of knowledge to make us too embarrassed to seek the answers we're looking for and we give up. But God tells us that if we seek Him we will find Him.

> *"Ask and it will be given to you; seek and you will find; knock and the door will be opened to you."*
>
> Matthew 7:7

How do we do that? There are several ways you can pursue God even when you don't understand.

- **Keep Reading.** Sometimes the passage will become clear when you read its full context.
- **Ask a Fellow Christian.** The Bible encourages us to seek wisdom from others. Ask a mentor, pastor or spiritually mature friend if they have any additional understanding of the passage in question. This can lead to great discussion and insight.
- **Use Study Guides & Resources.** Study Bibles have additional information about history, people, cultures, and meaning along with verse by verse breakdowns. These along with Bible commentaries are very helpful.
- **Join a Group.** We have several groups available for those who want to learn more about Jesus and the Bible. Alpha is a safe space for those exploring the basics of Christian faith in Jesus. READit is a 7-week class to help you learn to read and understand the Bible better.

If you're interested in gaining a better understanding of the Bible, joining a group, or learning more about growing your relationship with Jesus, please contact us.

 ALPHA

 READIT

Thoughts

1. Think about a Bible story or verse you've read that was hard to understand. Did you take any steps to try to understand what the passage meant? Why or why not?

2. Which of the suggestions above will you use the next time you're struggling to understand God's Word?

3. Write a prayer thanking God for meeting you where you are. Ask Him for clarity and understanding as you seek to know Him more.

---

[1]*Daniel 7:10*

Context: The angel reveals the meaning of Daniel's dream and God's eternal kingdom.

Earlier this week, we were reminded that Daniel didn't rely on his own understanding to decipher the dreams and visions God gave him. He always sought God's help. Even within his dream, he asks an angel to explain what he's seeing.

The angel explains that each beast represents a different earthly empire. When we compare Daniel's dream to King Nebuchadnezzar's, we begin to see the parallel. The lion with wings represents Babylon. The bear on its side with three ribs in its mouth symbolizes the Medo-Persian empire whose power was imbalanced. The leopard with four heads is thought to be Greece who conquered much of the civilized world in a very short amount of time under Alexander the Great. The empire was divided into four sections after his death. And the fourth beast, the one Daniel could only describe as terrifying and powerful, is believed to be Rome.

Empires, kings, and earthly leaders can be terrifying. They rule with unlimited power and authority. It appears nothing will be able to stop them. But as we learned this week, God Almighty, the Ancient of Days, sits on His throne. He too has a kingdom, one that will never end.

Daniel goes on to describe that the Ancient of Days, came and declared judgment over the beasts, or earthly rulers. In other words, God is giving us a spoiler alert to how everything will end, not just during Daniel's lifetime, but for all eternity. God will defeat every earthly ruler. He will establish His kingdom that will reign forever and nothing will be able to defeat Him.

It's easy to become disheartened when you rely on leaders, kings or governments for security. Because they are earthly kingdoms, they begin to fall as soon as they are built. But that isn't the case with God's kingdom. As followers of Jesus, we have hope and peace as we go through life because we know how the story ends. We can stand with confidence knowing that as quickly as God spoke goodness into the world, He will speak evil out of it.

> "I have told you these things, so that in me you may have peace. In this world you will have trouble. But take heart! I have overcome the world."
>
> John 16:33

1. Consider our world today. Where do you find your focus? Are you putting your trust in leaders, politicians and government?

2. God tells us to "take heart" which means "cheer up" because He has overcome the world. Examine your own emotions. Do you struggle to be hopeful?

3. Write a prayer to God. If necessary, confess when you've placed your trust in man's leadership rather than God's. Ask Him to replace your anxiety over the future with His peace.

GROUP STUDY GUIDE

Among Lions: ANCIENT OF DAYS

WEEK OF NOVEMBER 19, 2023

Synopsis:
Sometimes, when we study the end times in the Bible, we try to crack the code to figure out God's plans for the future. But God is not hiding anything from us—prophecy is supposed to reassure us. In Daniel 7, we learn about a visionary dream Daniel had that reminds us of the God we serve. The God of the furnace and the God of the lion's den is the same God who reigns over heaven and earth.

WARM UP QUESTION:
If you could spend a week anywhere in the world (with cost not being an obstacle), where would you go and what would you do there?

DISCUSS:

Read Daniel 7.

Split the reading between 2-3 people.

• Biblical scholars have come to conclude that the lion in Daniel's dream represents Babylon, the bear represents Medo-Persia, the leopard represents Greece, and the fourth beast represents Rome. After reading this Scripture and knowing the ultimate destinies of these four empires, what is most striking to you? What other observations do you have as you read about the beasts?

• Have one or two people reread verses 9-10, 13-14, 22, and 27. What characteristics do you see that describe the Ancient of Days? (Consider creating a list together.)

• Where do you see these characteristics of God at work today?

• Where do you struggle to see them today, and how do these verses encourage you in that struggle?

- This chapter paints a clear picture of earthly kingdoms versus an eternal kingdom. Would you say you tend to put your faith more in earthly kingdoms or an eternal one? How does this chapter challenge or inspire you to shift your viewpoint?

Read Hebrews 10:19-25 together out loud:

- What connections do you see between these verses and Daniel 7?

- Based on what these verses say about Jesus, or the "Son of Man," how are you encouraged to approach God differently than you do now?

- Of the specific actions that are mentioned in these verses, which one do you sense is most needed in your life?

RESPOND:
- What is one step you could take this week to put into practice what you've just discussed? When will you do it?

- Close your group time in prayer, thanking God for being the Ancient of Days who reigns over heaven and earth and who also invites you into His presence. Pray that each person would be faithful to follow through on the action steps they've just shared.

*Encourage group members to read Daily Bible Reading on the church app or have it delivered to their inbox daily. Subscribe at **www.thecrossinglv.com/app**. Check in with your group to share thoughts about these throughout the week!*

LEADER NOTES: Access to weekly message, podcast, & notes at *www.rightnowmedia.org*

Resources

Whether you need help with next steps, or know exactly what to do next, these resources are here to get you started. You can also email **connect@thecrossinglv.com** to get some 1 on 1 help with what's next for you.

TAKE THE NEXT STEP WITH JESUS

ROOTED

ALPHA

READIT

Made in the USA
Monee, IL
27 September 2023